CUTE & EASY *Oh Baby!* CAKE TOPPERS

Cute & Easy Cake Toppers for any Baby Shower, Christening, Birthday or Baby Celebration!

Contributors

Amanda Mumbray

Following a career in finance, Amanda Mumbray launched her cake business in 2010 and has gone from strength to strength, delighting customers with her unique bespoke creations and winning several Gold medals at various International Cake Shows. Amanda's **Clever Little Cupcake** company is based near Manchester, UK:
www.cleverlittlecupcake.co.uk

Kerry Rowe

Kerry Rowe is a keen hobby baker who enjoys making and baking cakes for family and friends and was a recent Gold medallist and winner at the UK Cake International Show.

Helen Penman

Helen Penman has been designing cakes for over 15 years and her work has been featured in a wide range of cake books and magazines. She has also written several cake decorating and modelling books of her own, and runs a successful cake company from her home in Kent, UK.
www.toonicetoslice.co.uk

Lesley Grainger

Lesley Grainger has been imaginative since birth and has baked since she was old enough to hold a spatula. When life-saving surgery prompted a radical rethink, Lesley left a successful corporate career to pursue her passion for cake making. Lesley is based in Greenock, Scotland. Say 'hello' at:
www.lesleybakescakes.co.uk

First published in 2014 by Kyle Craig Publishing

Text and illustration copyright © 2014 Kyle Craig Publishing

Editor: Alison McNicol

Design: Julie Anson

ISBN: 978-1-908-707-41-3

A CIP record for this book is available from the British Library.

A Kyle Craig Publication

www.kyle-craig.com

Contents

Welcome!

Welcome to **'Oh Baby!'**, the latest title in the **Cute & Easy Cake Toppers Collection.**

Each book in the series focuses on a specific theme, and here we have compiled a gorgeous selection of beautiful cake toppers that will be perfect for any baby shower, baby birthday, christening, naming ceremony or baby celebration!

Whether you're an absolute beginner or an accomplished cake decorator, these projects are suitable for all skill levels, and we're sure that you will have as much fun making them as we did!

Enjoy!

Fondant/Sugarpaste/Gumpaste

Fondant/Sugarpaste – Ready-made fondant, also called ready to roll icing, is widely available in a selection of fantastic colours. Most regular cake decorators find it cheaper to buy a larger quantity in white and mix their own colours using colouring pastes or gels. Fondant is used to cover entire cakes, and as a base to make modelling paste for modelling and figures (see below).

Modelling Paste – Used throughout this book. Firm but pliable and dries faster and harder than fondant/sugarpaste. When making models, fondant can be too soft so we add CMC/Tylose powder to thicken it.

Gumpaste – Also known as 'Florist Paste'. More pliable than fondant, but dries very quickly and becomes quite hard, so it is widely used for items like flowers that are delicate but need to hold their shape when dry. Gumpaste can be made by adding Gum-Tex/Gum Tragacanth to regular fondant.

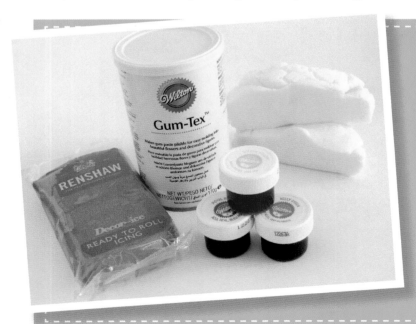

How to Make Modelling Paste

Throughout this book we refer to 'paste', meaning modelling paste. You can convert regular shop-bought fondant into modelling paste by adding CMC/Tylose powder, which is a thickening agent.

Add approx 1 tsp of CMC/Tylose powder to 225g (8oz) of fondant/sugarpaste. Knead well and leave in an airtight freezer bag for a couple of hours.

Add too much and it will crack. If this happens, add in a little shortening (white vegetable fat) to make it pliable again.

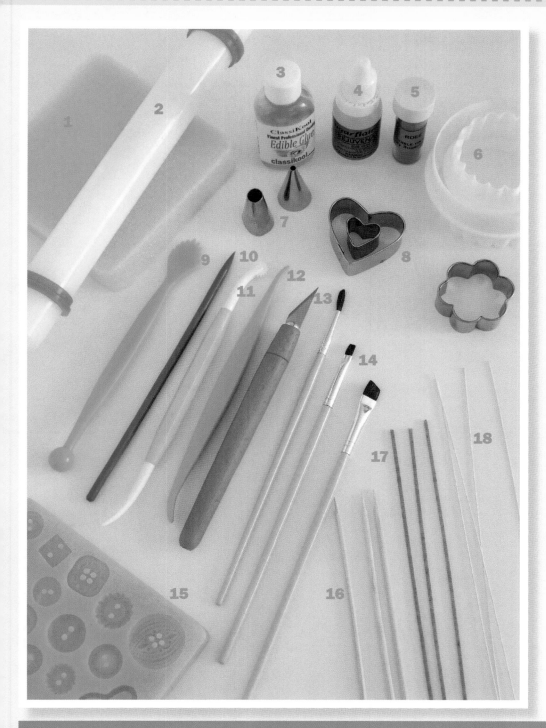

1 Foam Pad – holds pieces in place while drying.

2 Rolling pin – acrylic works better than wooden when working with fondant/paste.

3 Edible glue – essential when creating models. See below.

4 Rejuvenator spirit – mix with food colourings to create an edible paint.

5 Petal Dust, pink – for adding a 'blush' effect to cheeks.

6 Round and scalloped cutters – a modelling essential.

7 Piping nozzles – used to shape mouths and indents.

8 Shaped cutters – various uses.

9 Ball tool/serrated tool – another modelling essential.

10 Small pointed tool – used to create details like nostrils and holes.

11 Quilting tool – creates a stitched effect.

12 Veining tool – for adding details to flowers and models.

13 Craft knife/scalpel – everyday essential.

14 Brushes – to add finer details to faces.

15 Moulds – create detailed paste buttons, fairy wings and lots more.

16 Wooden skewers – to support larger models.

17 Spaghetti strands – also used for support.

18 Coated craft wire – often used in flower making.

Edible Glue

Whenever we refer to 'glue' in this book, we of course mean 'edible glue'. You can buy bottles of edible glue, which is strong and great for holding larger models together. You can also use a light brushing of water, some royal icing, or make your own edible glue by dissolving ¼ teaspoon tylose powder in 2 tablespoons warm water. Leave until dissolved and stir until smooth. This will keep for up to a week in the refrigerator.

Making Faces

The faces featured in this book vary in terms of detail and difficulty. If you're a complete beginner, you may wish to start with this very simple face technique. As your confidence grows, you can use fondant for eyes and pupils, edible paint for lashes and detailed eyes, or combine the two for some great detailing.

Simple Baby Face

 Roll a simple ball to start.

 The end of a piping nozzle makes a great smile.

 Add a tiny ball for nose.

 Use edible pens and/or fondant to add eye and hair details.

 A simple, tiny baby is born!

Detailed Face

 A veining or ball tool will create indents for features.

 White fondant forms the main eye.

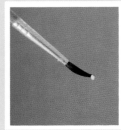 When adding tiny pieces of fondant for eyes, use a moist fine brush.

 Fine black fondant creates lashes.

 Edible paint creates more detail and pink petal dust adds blush to cheeks.

Cupcake Toppers

When making small figures for cupcakes, it's great to place each on a topper disc, and place this on top of a lovely swirl of buttercream. This way the figure can be removed and kept, allowing guests to tuck into the main cupcake.

Regular round cutters are essentials, and there are also a great selection of embossing tools and sheets out there that, when pressed into your rolled paste, will create cool quilting effects on your disc. Make your discs first and allow them to harden before you fix your figures to them.

You can also combine a scalloped cutter with the point of a small, round piping nozzle to create discs with cut-out holes.

Plunger cutters are a great way to add cute details to your models. They cut and then 'push' each small piece out, making it easy to cut small flowers, leaves and shapes.

Using the Quilting Tool

The quilting tool is a small wheel with spikes that, when rolled across fondant or paste creates a cute 'stitched' effect. It can be used for so many lovely details:

Facial features on 'toys'.

Detailing on small shapes.

Quilted blanket effect.

Materials

Modelling paste:
Egg yellow, Baby pink,
Dark pink, Flesh,
Baby blue, Lilac,
Black, Green,
White, Red,
Food colouring: white
Petal dust: pink
Rejuvenator spirit
Edible glue

Tools

Craft knife/scalpel
Wooden skewer
Veining tool
Small fluted cutter
Circle cutter
Flower plunger cutter
Piping tip
Cone tool
Paintbrush

1 Roll out two sausages for the legs. With the cone tool or end of a paintbrush, insert into one end to open up the ends.

2 Place the legs on a cake dummy, and insert a skewer to support the body.

3 Insert cocktail sticks into the bottom of the legs to hold the shoes in place.

4 Roll out a large cone shape for the boddy.

5 Indent at the top, and pinch out strap details. Shape the tummy until you're happy with the pregnant bump shape.

6 Slide the tummy shape through the skewer, with some edible glue in place, and position over the legs.

7 Form a small piece of flesh paste for the chest area and slide over the skewer, gluing in place.

8 Using a small cutter, use the fluted side to make a disc.

9 Cut out the centre using a smaller circle cutter, and cut to open it up.

10 Place the scallop around the neckline.

11 Roll a ball for the head and place on the shoulders.

12 Add a small nose and ears, indenting with the cone tool to give definition.

13 Using the small end of the ball tool, indent eye sockets, and using a piping tip make a mark for the mouth.

14 Open up the mouth.

15 Add two small white oval pieces for the eyes.

16 Add a very small piece of pink to fill in the mouth, and an even smaller piece of white to make the teeth.

17 Roll two very small tapered black sausages for the eyelashes, kicking them up at the edges.

18 Paint in the eyes with paste colours mixed with rejuvenator spirit.

19 Dust the cheeks with a little petal dust.

20 Cut a thin strip and wrap around the top of the tummy bump.

21 Cut out the above shape with a craft knife.

22 Fold both edges into the centre. Glue in place.

23 Cut a small strip and wrap and glue around the centre to finish off the bow.

24 Cut two strips for the bow tails and glue in place.

25 Glue the bow on the tummy, and paint polka dots on the top to add extra detail.

26 Roll out a sausage for each arm, indenting slightly for the wrist and elbow.

27 Flatten the hand, and cut out a section to make a thumb.

28 Make three further cuts to make the fingers.

29 Attach the arms with glue, one gently sitting on her lap, the other on top of her baby bump.

30 Roll out a very long thin sausage to make the hair.

31 Cut sections off, and taper at the ends.

32 Wet the head, and start arranging the hair on the head.

33 Continue to attach the hair until all the head is covered.

34 Make a few smaller sausages to soften the front of the hair. Make a smaller bow like, like before, for the top and glue to head.

35 Roll out two teardrop shapes for the shoes. Flatten slightly.

36 Attach the shoes to the exposed cocktail sticks at the end of each leg.

37 Roll out a cone shape for the bouquet.

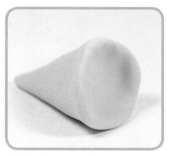

38 Hollow out slightly at the large end.

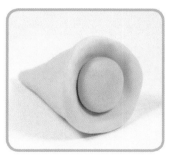

39 Roll out a ball, flatten it, and glue into the top of the bouquet shape.

40 Cut out lots of flowers using the plunger cutter, adding flattened balls of paste to the centres. Glue in place.

41 Make little leaves out of tiny flattened teardrop shapes. Add detail with the veining tool.

42 Paint little polka dots on the bouquet wrapper.

43 Make a tapered cone and flatten slightly. Mark the sides to look like a cupcake.

44 Roll a long sausage to make the cupcake frosting. Start to wind the sausage shape up like a spiral.

45 Keep winding until it looks like frosting.

46 Roll a tiny ball for the little cherry.

Materials

Modelling paste:

Pink

Baby blue

Flesh

Brown (pinch)

White fondant/cupcakes

Edible pen: brown

Petal dust: pink

Edible glue

Tools

Craft knife/scalpel

Veining tool

Scalloped cutters: small and large

Small star plunger cutter

Piping nozzle (any)

1 Start by covering the required number of cupcakes with white fondant. Adding buttercream beneath will keep the cakes moist.

2 Roll a small ball of flesh paste for the baby's head.

3 Indent a smile using the back of any piping nozzle.

4 Roll a tiny ball for the nose and glue in place.

5 Roll two small ovals for the baby's hands.

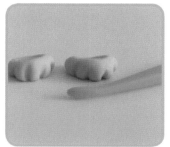

6 Use the veining tool to indent the shape of the fingers.

7 Roll two tiny balls of brown paste for the eyes and a tiny teardrop for the hair. Indent and glue onto head. Add tiny eyebrow details with edible pen.

8 For the baby bib, cut a small scalloped circle, then remove a section, as shown.

9 Add a tiny star to the bib.

10 For the blanket, cut a larger scalloped circle.

11 Add lots of tiny stars to the blanket and glue in place.

12 Rather than add a baby to every single cupcake, mix it up with some other baby accessories, or glue one of these in front of the baby.

13 See pages 17-19 for baby accessories. Why not add a dummy/pacifier...

14 ...or a baby bottle?!

Cute Baby

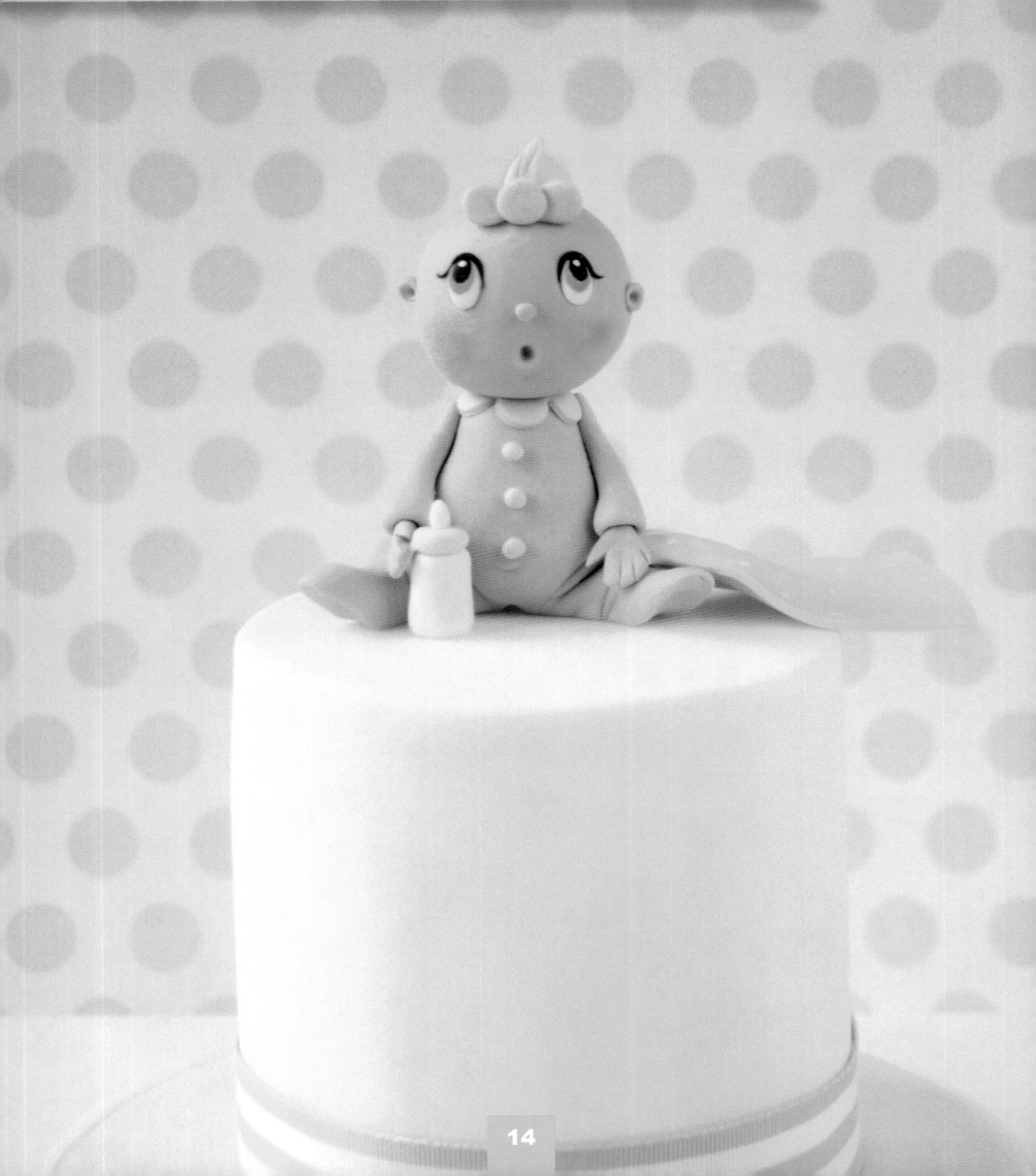

Materials

Modelling paste:
Green
Pink
Flesh
Black
Yellow
Food colouring: white, blue
Rejuvenator spirit
Edible glue

Tools

Craft knife/scalpel
Toothpick
Veining tool
Bulbous cone tool
Taper cone tool
Flower/blossom cutter
Fine paintbrush

1 Roll an elongated egg shape with green modelling paste.

2 Make a cut to start shaping the legs.

3 Shape the legs and pinch a foot shape. Using a veining tool, make indentations around the legs to suggest movement. Insert a toothpick for the head.

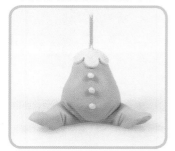

4 Cut a blossom out of contrasting modelling paste to make the collar of the baby suit and add tiny balls for the buttons.

5 Roll a large ball out of flesh paste, adding small balls for the ears and nose. Indent into the ears slightly to give definition. Indent with ball tool to make eye sockets.

6 Roll out two small egg shaped white balls, flattening slightly. Insert into the eye sockets, using edible glue.

7 Roll out two tiny black sausages for the eyelashes, flicking up slightly at the outer edge. Indent a hole with end of a paintbrush to make the mouth.

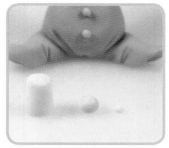

8 Roll a small cylinder in white, small pink ball and tiny white ball. Flatten the pink ball and place on top of cylinder, and place white ball on top to make the bottle teat.

9 Roll two small teardrops and a small ball to make the bow. Flatten them all. Make a small teardrop for hair, and add detail with veining tool.

10 Glue bow and hair in place, and place the bottle in front of the baby. Mix rejuvenator spirit with food colouring to make paint, and paint in eye details.

11 For the arms, roll two sausages and open up the sleeve ends with the cone tool. For the hands, roll out a teardrop shape, flatten, then cut in the finger details with knife.

12 Glue the arms to the baby's body, arranging one on the bottle.

13 To make the blanket, cut a rectangle of paste, and concertina one edge.

14 Paint some polka dots on to the blanket, and place the blanket under the baby's other hand.

1 Start by cutting a selection of sugarpaste discs for your tiny toppers to sit on. One for each cupcake. Set aside to dry.

2 Roll out a tiny circle with the smallest pastry cutter, pulling it slightly at each side to make it oval.

3 Roll out a sausage, slightly thicker at one end, and cut where it starts to taper in.

4 Attach the teat shape to the oval. Set aside to dry for a few hours.

5 Once dry, roll a sausage and attach to the bottom of the dummy/pacifier to make the handle.

6 For the bib you can use the *Autumn Carpenter Baby Cookie Cutters* or the tiny template on page 49.

7 Roll out the paste, and place the texture sheet over the top. Carefully roll over it with your rolling pin to make the impression.

8 Using the bib shaped cutter, cut out the shape. Or cut a bib shape using the template and add details using your existing modelling tools.

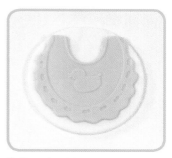

9 Glue the bib to a disc of sugarpaste.

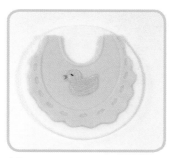

10 Paint in the duck detail with food colouring.

11 Again, you may cut a onesie using the template from page 49 if you do not have the cutter set.

12 Roll out the paste, and place the texture sheet over the top. Roll over it as in step 7.

13 Cut out the onesie shape with the cutter.

14 Place it on a disc of sugarpaste.

15 Paint on the detail with food colouring mixed with rejuvenator spirit.

16 The nappy/diaper pin requires no special cutters!

17 Roll out a long sausage of paste.

18 Make the pin shape by looping it in the middle, and cutting off the excess.

19 Roll out a ball of paste, flatten it slightly, and cut out a V shape.

20 Assemble the pin on a disc of sugarpaste.

21 ABC blocks are cute and simple to make!

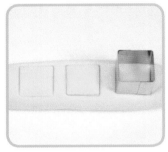

22 Roll out a large, flat sausage of paste, and indent with a square cutter, if you have one (do not go all the way through the paste).

23 Using a sharp knife, cut out the blocks so they are nice and sharp.

24 Assemble the blocks on the sugarpaste disc.

25 Paint in the letter and stitching details.

26 Hello duckie!

27 Roll out a fat sausage, tapering at one end and roll in the middle to thin slightly.

28 Bend the head back, and lift the tail up.

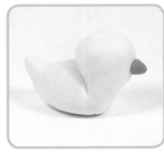

29 Attach a small cone shape for the beak.

30 Attach to the sugarpaste disc, paint the eyes on, and dust the cheeks with a little petal dust.

31 Baby rattle toy!

32 Roll out a ball of paste.

33 Cut out a circle of paste, and glue the ball to the top.

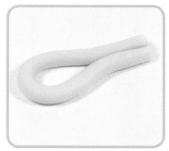

34 Make a loop out of a thin sausage of paste.

35 Make a hole underneath the rattle head with the end of a paintbrush.

36 Glue this handle in place and attach to the sugarpaste disc.

37 A baby bottle makes a cute and easy cupcake topper or cake accessory!

38 Make a cylinder of paste.

39 Cut out a circle of paste and attach it to the top.

40 Roll out a tiny ball of paste to make the teat.

41 Attach it to the sugarpaste disc, and paint on the bottle markings.

42 Every baby needs a teddy bear!

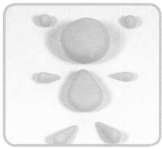

43 Roll a large teardrop shape for body, ball for head, two small balls for ears, and four teardrop shapes for arms and legs (arms slightly smaller than legs).

44 Glue all the parts together, indenting the ears with a ball tool.

45 Attach a circle of paste for the muzzle in a slightly lighter shade. Run the quilting tool up the centre, indent mouth with the end of a paintbrush.

46 Add a small ball for the nose and attach to the disc. Add the eyes, and dust the cheeks with a little petal dust.

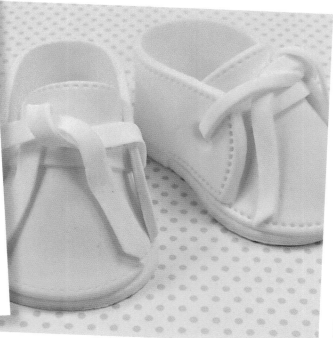

Materials

Modelling paste:

White

Baby pink

Baby blue

Egg yellow

Green

Cream

Edible glue

Tools

Templates:
pages 48 and 49
Craft knife/scalpel
Cone tool
Veining tool
Quilting tool
Star cutters
Blossom, leaf and circle cutters (optional)
Paintbrush

1 Use the templates to cut out the 3 shoe parts. Use quilting tool around outer edge of upper pieces to apply 'stitch' detail.

2 Apply a layer of edible glue around edge of sole of shoe. For all shoes except laced up version, glue heel piece then front piece to sole.

3 Use veining tool to gently push upper pieces into place. Leave shoes to dry until they are firm to touch. You can insert a small piece of foam to retain shape while drying.

4 For the flower design, use the small templates or cutters to cut out flower and leaf shapes.

5 Using the cone tool, punch dots around the outer edges of each piece to suggest stitching (optional). Position and affix pieces onto each shoe with edible glue.

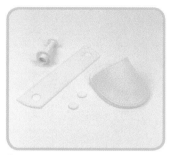

6 To create the laced up style, cut a hole at either end using the circle cutter. Affix the toe piece to the sole before attaching this heel piece.

7 Cut 2 x 250mm (10in) length strips of white paste to form the shoelaces, using a strip cutter or sharp knife. Carefully thread each lace through the eyelets.

8 Arrange the shoelaces in a loose 'tie' instead of attempting a bow! Affix the end of each shoelace to the body of the shoe with edible glue.

9 Roll a thick piece of white paste, and cut small circles from a contrasting piece using a circle cutter or nozzle end. Place the circles on top of the white paste.

10 Roll your rolling pin across the attached dots, flattening them into the white paste. Cut with the smaller star cutter. Cut a larger star from a contrasting colour.

11 Use the quilting tool to create detail, as desired. Place the smaller star on top of the larger one and glue to shoe.

12 Use the small template from page 49, or a knife and fluted cutter, to cut out the cupcake pieces.

13 Use a small fluted cutter to cut the frosting part, then roll a small bead of paste to form the cherry on top!

14 Using the quilting tool, create detail on the cupcake case, as shown. Glue all pieces to the shoes.

Jack in the Box

Materials

Modelling paste:

White, Ivory,

Baby blue, Mid blue,

Flesh, Light brown,

Black

Petal dust: pink

Crispie treats or
styrene cube

Edible glue

Tools

Craft knife/scalpel
Piece of card: 7.6 cm
(3in) square
Spaghetti strands
Lollipop stick
Veining tool
Ball tool
Quilting tool
Fondant smoother
Patchwork embosser
Small heart cutter

1 Start with a large egg of white paste to shape the body, place two pieces of spaghetti through to support the head and the arms.

2 Shape two white cylinders to form the arms, glue these in place over the spaghetti.

3 Roll blue paste into a long, thin sausage shape, then continue to roll with the smoother.

4 First paint glue all over the body then, starting from the bottom, begin to wrap the rolled paste around the body. Alternate colours and hide joins at the back.

5 Continue the same process on the arms.

6 Using a piece of ivory paste roll and shape to form the head and shape a mouth using the veining tool.

7 Roll thin sausages of light brown paste, cut and glue to head. Start from the bottom of the hairline and work around and upwards.

8 Roll 2 balls of ivory paste for the hands. Flatten slightly. Cut then shape the fingers. Slide onto spaghetti and glue each hand in place.

9 Roll a small ball for the nose. Roll then indent balls for the ears. Glue in place.

10 Use tiny amounts of black and white paste to form the eyes, glue into place.

11 Roll and cut out a rectangular and triangular shape for the hat. Use the quilting tool to add details to the edge of the rectangular piece.

12 Wrap the triangle around a support and glue slightly (it does not have to seal fully). Wrap the rectangular piece around the bottom of the hat. Leave to dry before attaching.

13 Roll and indent a small oval for the tongue, glue in place. Dust cheeks, nose, tongue and ears with petal dust.

14 When the hat is dry, make four small balls of the darker blue and glue into place, when completely dry glue the hat onto the head.

Jack's Box

1 Make a 7.6 cm (3in) square cube by covering a cake, rice crispie treat or polystyrene in white fondant. Do not worry about the finish as all sides will be covered.

2 Start by gluing Jack into place.

3 Roll blue paste into a long sausage with fingers, then continue to roll with the smoother. Glue and place this around the base of the cube.

4 Roll and cut 4 pieces of white paste each 8.9cm (3.5in) square for the sides and 1 piece 7.6cm (3in) square for the lid. Use the patchwork embosser to mark all five pieces.

5 Allow these pieces to dry for as long as possible, then glue front and back panels only into place.

6 Glue the sides into place; you may find that these may need a slight trim to fit.

7 Roll four balls of white paste for the feet of the box, flatten slightly and place a piece of cocktail stick in each. Put aside to dry and harden.

8 Roll lots of small balls of blue paste and glue into place on the joins of the patchwork.

9 Decorate the lid with balls of blue paste and trim with rolled fondant.

10 Using blue rolled fondant trim down the sides and across the top of the box and glue in place.

11 Glue the lid at its base onto the box and lean it up against Jack. If Jack is completely dry and set then he will support it, add glue to his back where it is not visible.

12 Take the hardened feet, brush with glue then lift box onto feet.

13 Finish the box off by using rolled out blue fondant. Use this stage to cover any gaps, marks or joins to give a better finish.

14 You now have Jack in his box, ready to add to any cake!

Elephant

1 Start with a ball of blue paste and shape to form the body. Place a small piece of spaghetti through the center to hold the head in place.

2 Roll out two pieces of blue paste. Form a teardrop shape, using the ball tool to press to shape the feet. Glue onto the body.

3 Repeat step 2 to form the arms. Glue onto the body.

4 Roll a ball of blue paste to form the head.

5 Use fingers to form the shape of a trunk.

6 Use four pieces of ivory paste to form the pads of the feet. Press flat and glue into place.

7 Use small pieces of ivory paste rolled into a ball and flattened to form the toes for the feet and hands, glue into place.

8 Using the pointing tool mark a stitched effect down the trunk, arms and legs.

9 For the ears, start with two balls of blue and two smaller balls of ivory paste.

10 Roll these out into flat ovals. Glue the ivory onto the blue paste.

11 Shape the ears with fingers by pinching at one end.

12 Glue the ears into place and shape until desired shape is achieved.

13 Make the eyes with tiny amounts of black and white paste and glue onto the face.

14 Your little elephant is now complete!

Giraffe

1 Roll a tall, oval cylinder shape of blue paste for the body, and insert a piece of spaghetti to support the head.

2 Roll two legs, shaping into a teardrop shape, and attach to the body with the edible glue.

3 Follow step 2 for the arms. Shape and glue in place.

4 Roll more blue paste into a slight oblong shape for the head.

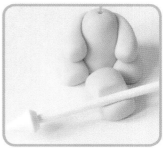

5 Roll the handle of the pointing tool to shape the nose and eye area. Use edible glue to attach to the body over the piece of spaghetti.

6 Using two small pieces each of both blue and ivory paste, shape as shown to make the horns. Glue into place.

7 Take a small circle of blue paste and slightly smaller circle of ivory paste.

8 Place the ivory on top of the blue paste with a tiny amount of glue and press down slightly to shape. Cut in half.

9 Pinch the two ends together, use a tiny amount of glue to keep in place.

10 Glue ears in place underneath the giraffe's horns.

11 Use the pointing tool to make the giraffe's nostrils and to add a 'stitched' effect to the arms and legs.

12 Take two tiny amounts each of black and white paste. Use to make the eyes and glue into place.

13 Use icing nozzles to cut out circles to use as pads for the feet and hands and spots on the body.

14 Your baby giraffe is now complete!

1 Roll a short oval cylinder shape of blue paste for the body, and insert a piece of spaghetti to support the head.

2 Roll out two balls of blue paste and flatten slightly for the feet/paws, attach to the body with the edible glue.

3 Roll out two small lengths of blue paste for the arms. Shape into a teardrop shape and glue to body.

4 Roll a ball shape for the head. Attach using a small amount of glue over the spaghetti.

5 Use the quilting tool to mark down the middle of the head, body, arms and legs.

6 Using two small and six smaller pieces of ivory, flatten and glue onto the bottom of the feet to form pads.

7 Take a small amount of ivory to form the muzzle and black to make the nose, shape into a triangle and glue into place.

8 Take two tiny white and black balls to make the eyes, glue into place.

9 For the ears, roll two balls of blue and two smaller balls of ivory. Flatten and glue together.

10 Pinch the bottom of the ears together as shown and use a craft knife to cut off surplus and create a smooth line for gluing onto the head.

11 Glue into place on top of the head.

12 Cut out a triangular shape from a rolled out piece of blue paste.

13 Roll into a conical shape for a hat. Glue together then onto the teddy's head and finish with an ivory band and a tiny ivory ball.

14 Hello tiny teddy!

The Toys

1 Roll and cut a strip of blue paste to make the book cover and a thicker piece of white paste to make the pages.

2 Using a sharp knife cut into the white paste to make the pages of the book.

3 Glue and fold the cover onto the pages and cut and glue a small heart to front cover of book.

4 Use the pointing tool to mark around the edge of the book.

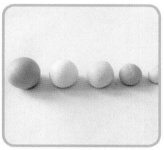

5 Take different coloured balls of paste in decreasing sizes.

6 Flatten the largest ball to make the base, take a piece of pop stick and place this into the centre of the flattened paste.

7 Repeat the process, flattening each ball, and use an icing nozzle to make a hole in the centre of each. Place over stick, gluing into place.

8 For the last hoop use a small nozzle to make a hole, glue into place.

9 Roll several ivory coloured balls.

10 Using the smoother square off the edges.

11 Continue on the remaining number of balls, squaring each.

12 Using a piece of coloured paste, roll out very thinly.

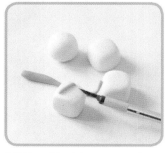

13 Use this thin paste to form letters and glue onto cubes.

14 The toys are now ready to add to your cake!

Little Bear

Materials

Modelling paste:

Light brown

Pink

Flesh

Baby blue

Black (pinch)

Petal dust: pink

Edible glue

Tools

Craft knife/scalpel

Toothpick

Ball tool

Quilting tool

Plunger circle cutter

1 Roll a teardrop shape for the body and insert a toothpick ready to take the head.

2 Roll out a tapered sausage shape, and indent paw markings with the back of the craft knife. Make 2.

3 Glue both legs in place.

4 For the arms, roll and indent two more sausage shapes, slightly smaller than the legs, and attach to the body.

5 Roll out a large ball for the head and insert on to the toothpick.

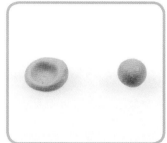

6 Roll out two small balls of paste, and indent with the small end of the ball tool.

7 Glue each ear to the sides of the head.

8 To make the muzzle, cut a circle from flesh coloured paste. Pull it at the sides to make it slightly oval, and glue in place.

9 Run the quilting wheel up the middle of the muzzle, and indent a mouth with the end of a paintbrush.

10 Make a nose with a small ball of black paste and glue in place.

11 Paint on the eyes, and dust the cheeks with pink petal dust.

12 To make the bow, roll out two teardrop shapes, and a small ball for the centre. Flatten it, and arrange into a bow shape.

13 Glue the bow to the head in front of the ear.

14 Play around with different colours for the bow to suit the theme of your cake.

Little Bunny

Materials

Modelling paste:

Pink, Dark pink,
Baby blue, Egg yellow

Black

Petal Dust: pink

Food colours: white,
black

Rejuvenator spirit

Edible glue

Tools

Craft knife/scalpel

Toothpick

1 Roll out a teardrop shape and insert a toothpick ready to take the head.

2 Roll out two teardrop shapes and flatten slightly.

3 Attach the legs to the front of the body as shown.

4 Roll out a sausage and taper slightly at each end.

5 Insert the sausage through the toothpick, so it sits on top of the body.

6 Roll a ball and insert onto the toothpick. Secure with edible glue.

7 Make two holes on the top of the head with the end of a paintbrush. These will take the ears.

8 Make two small teardrop shapes, flattening slightly, and insert into the holes, glue in place.

9 Cut out contrasting baby blue pieces for the ears, feet and chest with a sharp knife, and glue in place.

10 Make a little dark pink nose and glue in place.

11 To make the bow, roll out two dark pink teardrop shapes and a small ball, flatten slightly, and arrange into a bow shape.

12 Glue the bow to the bunny. Add the eyes, and brush a little petal dust on the cheeks.

13 Mix white food colour with rejuvenator spirit to make white paint and paint some polka dots to the chest, ears and feet.

14 Play around with different colours to suit the theme of your cake.

Materials

Modelling paste:
Baby pink
Dark pink
Baby blue
Egg yellow
Brown
Black
Petal dust: pink
Rejuvenator spirit
Edible glue

Tools

Craft knife/scalpel
Quilting tool
Ball tool
Small heart cutter
Blossom plunger cutter
Circle plunger cutter
Paintbrush

1 Cut or copy the bunny template from page 49 and lay over rolled out modelling paste.

2 Using a craft knife, carefully cut around and through the paste to cut the bunny head

3 Make a little heart shaped nose.

4 Cut teardrop shapes for the ears. Glue all in place.

5 Paint on the facial details and dust the cheeks with petal dust.

6 Cut out a flower with the plunger cutter, and cup by rolling the ball tool around the centre of the flower.

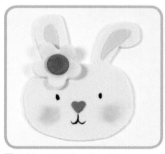

7 Add a ball for the flower centre and attach to the bunny's head.

8 Use the template on page 49 for the teddy bear's head and cut out using the craft knife.

9 Cut out a smaller circle, and elongate slightly by pulling at each side.

10 Run the stitching wheel up the centre of the muzzle and use the end of a paintbrush to make a mouth.

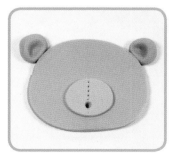

11 To make the ears, roll two small balls and indent with the ball tool. Glue in place.

12 Add a black nose.

13 To make the bow, roll two teardrop shapes, and a small ball, flatten, and arrange into a bow shape.

14 Glue the bow to the bear's head. Paint in the facial details and dust the cheeks with a little petal dust.

Double Trouble!

Materials

Modelling paste:
Flesh
Yellow
Green
Pink
Baby blue
White
Black
Petal dust: pink
Edible pen: black
Edible glue

Tools

Craft Knife/scalpel
Toothpicks
Spaghetti strands
Foam pads
Veining tool
Ball tool
Quilting tool
Paintbrush

1 Shape the body from flesh paste, insert a strand of spaghetti into the top to support the head. Leave to dry.

2 Shape the legs with foot and ankle and bend at right angles. Girl baby has two bent legs, boy one bent and one straight. Glue legs to bodies.

3 For nappy/diaper shape two white oval shapes, flatten and score using veining tool. Wrap around where the legs join to the body.

4 Shape more white paste into a rough triangle, score and texture as before. Glue in place between legs.

5 For the arms, shape two sausages, then flatten hand section and thin wrist, bend and glue to body. Hold in position with foam until dry.

6 Roll an oval for the head. Indent the mouth, add a tiny ball for a nose. Flatten and shape two slightly larger balls for the ears.

7 Indent then add two tiny white balls for eyes, then two tiny black balls for the pupils.

8 Add blush to the cheeks with pink petal dust.

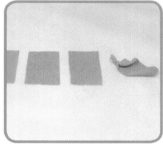

9 For the girl's blanket roll and cut a pink rectangle. Use quilting tool around the edge. Gather one corner and glue to baby's hand.

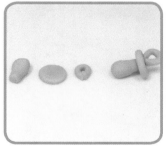

10 Shape a teardrop then cut off pointed end. Attach to a small circle of paste. Roll a tiny thin sausage, loop and glue in place.

11 Roll a white cylinder for the bottle. Shape a little disc, a small dome and a tiny ball for the tip of the teat. Attach each with edible glue.

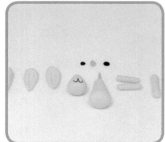

12 Shape an oval for the bunny body, a head, two arms, two legs and two long ears. Paint on face and add nose and eyes. Glue to baby boy.

13 For the big pink bow, roll paste thinly and cut a long strip. Fold each end to the centre, support with foam until dry.

14 Finish the bow with another strip of paste, fold over the central join and glue in place. Attach to the baby head with more edible glue.

Materials

Modelling paste:
Dark brown
Flesh
Green
Yellow
Pink
Edible pen: black
Petal dust: pink
Edible glue

Tools

Craft knife/scalpel
Toothpick
Small scissors
Ball tool
Veining tool
Medium heart cutter
Small flower cutter
Paintbrush

1 With dark brown paste, form an egg shape which will become the body of your monkey. For the head, roll a ball approx. half the size of the body.

2 Insert a toothpick through the centre of the body, leaving some free to support the head. Allow both the head and body to dry slightly before joining together.

3 Wait until the parts are dry enough so that the body can support the head. Place head onto the toothpick and connect with edible glue.

4 Roll flesh paste thinly and cut an egg shape large enough to cover the torso of your monkey. Additionally, cut a heart shape then remove the pointed bottom half.

5 Shape an oval pad of flesh paste, approx. half the height of your monkey's head. Use veining tool to create a mouth. Roll a small oval of dark brown for the nose. Glue in place.

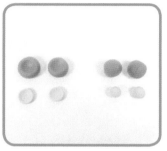

6 For the ears, roll 2 x balls of dark brown and 2 x small of flesh paste. Use your ball tool to create indentations into each piece.

7 Use edible glue to attach the ears, as pictured.

8 For the legs, roll two sausage shaped pieces of dark brown paste, approx. the same length as your monkey's body.

9 Using your thumb and forefinger, roll the sausage shape into a golf tee shape. Use a large ball tool to create a shallow cavity on one end.

10 Roll 2 x balls of flesh paste for the feet. Press each gently into a flat shape and using your scalpel tool, cut 4 'toes'. Pull the foot up a little at the back.

11 Bending the legs at the knee area, glue to either side of the body. Insert the foot piece into the cavity created by the ball tool. Repeat steps 8-11 for the arms/hands.

12 Add eyes with the edible pen. Use a veining tool to create eyebrows and dust petal dust on cheeks. Make three small snips into the head to create tufts of 'hair'.

13 Roll a thin sausage of green paste. Cut a flower shape and roll a small ball of yellow. Arrange the flower and and attach with edible glue.

14 Your monkey is complete! You can also make him in lovely pastel colours if this fits the theme of your baby cake better!

1 For each teddy, create a body which is largely egg shaped but flat at the base. Roll a ball shape for the head. Allow to dry.

2 For the arms and legs, take four equal size balls of paste. Roll these into sausage shapes which taper slightly at one end.

3 Shape each 'limb' by pinching the widest part into a flat 'foot' shape. Insert a toothpick into the centre of the body and add the head, using edible glue.

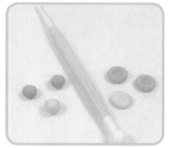

4 For the ears, roll 2 x brown coloured balls and shape using ball tool. For the snout, roll 1 x flesh coloured ball and flatten between finger and thumb.

5 Using edible glue, attach the arms, legs, snout and ears. Roll a small ball of black paste for the nose, and glue in place.

6 Add flesh accents to the ears and feet. Use the veining tool to create a smile and tummy button. Add the eyes and dust cheeks with petal dust.

7 For the crown, roll and cut a thin rectangle of paste. Cut out small triangles. For the gift, make a small cube and cut thin strips to form the ribbons.

8 Glue seam of the crown at the back and assemble the gift, allow to dry for a little while. Attach to the bear with edible glue.

9 For the female bear, follow all of the previous steps but add pretty little eyelashes. Cut two small rectangles of pink paste, as shown, to create a bow.

10 Make a pretty bunch of flowers by cutting thin strips of green paste, wrapping one around the others. Cut a selection of tiny sugarpaste blossoms.

11 Attach the 'bunch' to the teddy's tummy and add the tiny blossoms to complete the look. Fix the bow to the teddy's head.

12 To create a 'ragged' teddy look, make the teddy in the same way as outlined however use small sharp scissors to give texture.

13 Make the teddy's blanket by using the quilting wheel tool to make a border around a square of paste, then a quilted crisscross pattern.

14 Fold the top of the blanket to create the impression that it is being 'held' by the bear. Attach to the figure using edible glue.

Baby Elephant

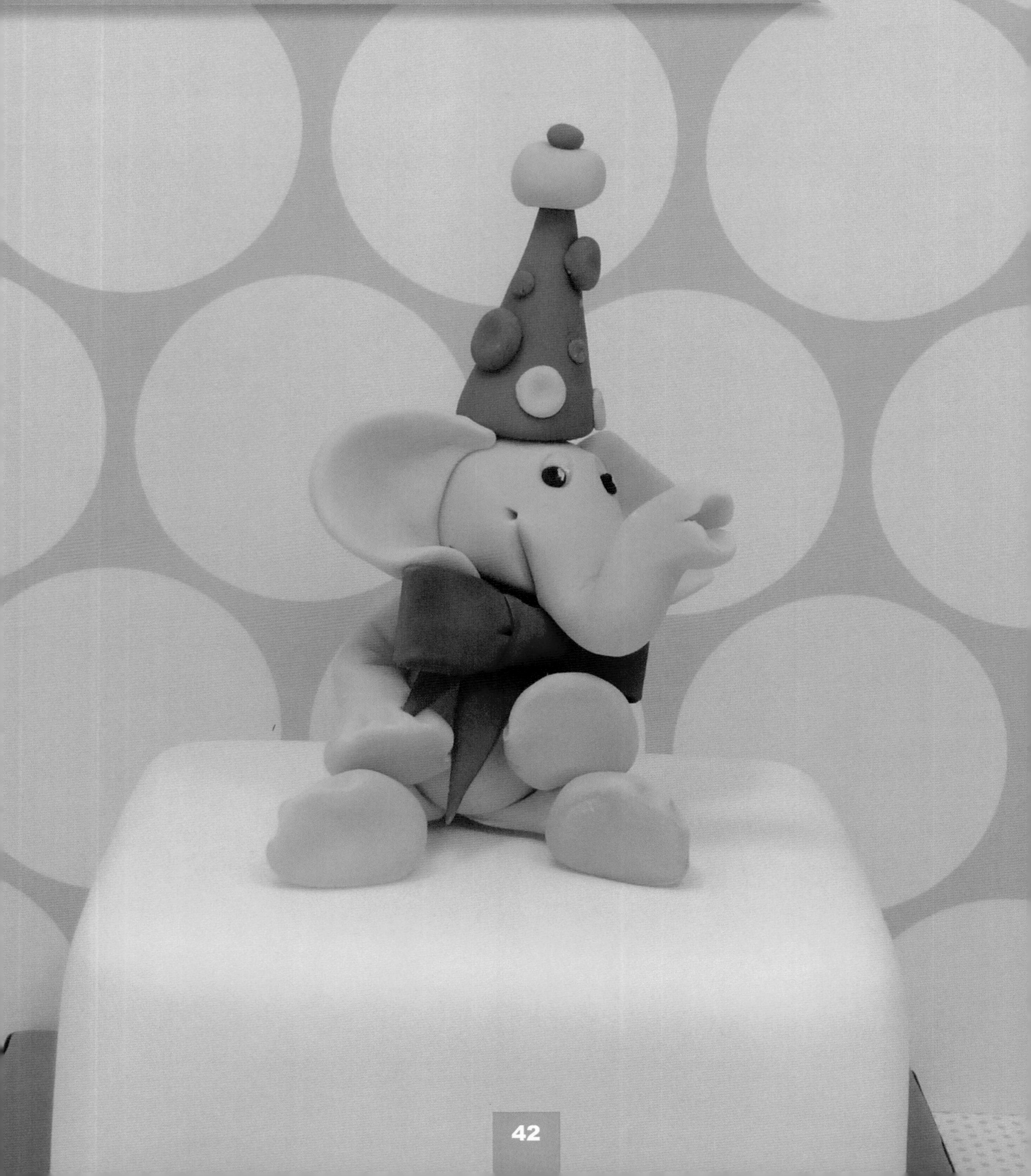

Materials

Modelling paste:

Green

Red

Blue

Black & white (pinch)

Edible glue

Tools

Craft knife/scalpel

Spaghetti strands

Toothpicks

Mini palette knife

Veining tool

Ball tool

1 Roll a green pear shape for the body, and insert a spaghetti strand into the top to support the head.

2 Shape two legs, leaving the base of each broad for the feet. Indent the ends for the nails detail. Tuck the narrow ends under the body and glue in place.

3 For the head, roll a large teardrop shape and thin out the pointed end to create a trunk.

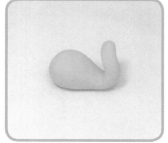

4 Bend the trunk up and forwards, opening the end of the trunk with the veining tool. Support the trunk in this position with foam and leave to dry.

5 Indent the eyes with the small ball tool then add small balls of white fondant to start the eyes. Indent the mouth using veining tool.

6 Add two tiny dots of black onto the white eyes. Add a little white dot onto the black eyes, this adds depth and makes them more realistic.

7 Shape the front legs. Roll into a teardrop, thinning the narrow end, indent the toes as before and glue to the top of the body. Glue head on top of body.

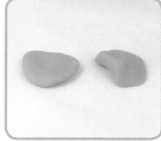

8 Start each ear with a triangle, thin the pointed end and fatten the broad end then make into a curved shape. Make two, support with foam until set.

9 For the hat, roll red paste into a long cone. Roll various sized small balls to decorate. Flatten then glue the balls to hat.

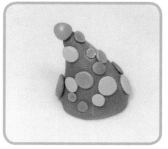

10 Add a larger ball for the pom pom on the top of the hat.

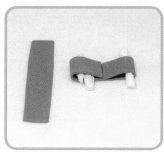

11 For the bow, roll paste thinly, and cut a long thin strip. Fold edges into centre of the strip to form two loops. Support loops with foam until dried.

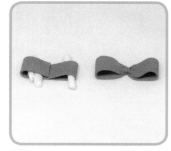

12 Whilst the bow is still soft, pinch the centre together where the two ends meet, making the pinched centre part of the bow. Use the veining tool to do this.

13 Cut another strip of red paste for the middle of the bow. Dampen and wrap around pinched-in centre of bow. Trim to neaten.

14 Cut out a red square then cut across it diagonally to make two tails for the bow. Glue these in place first, then glue the bow over the top, as shown.

Babyface Cupcakes

Materials

Modelling paste:
Flesh
Baby pink
Baby blue
Light brown
Black (pinch)
White non-pareils
Petal dust: pink
Edible pen: brown
Edible glue

Tools

Craft knife/scalpel
Toothpicks
Foam cupcake dome formers
Veining tool
Quilting tool
78mm (3in) round cutter
Medium daisy cutter
Paintbrush

1 Use the round cutter to cut out one disc of flesh paste per cupcake. Shape over the top of your foam formers and allow to dry until slightly firm.

2 Take a little bunch of toothpicks and secure tightly with an elastic band.

3 Roll out a piece of paste thinly and large enough to accommodate 2 x 78mm (3in) circles. Do not cut the circles – simply make a light indentation with the cutter on one side.

4 Using a toothpick bunch, stamp the paste firmly enough to create texture. Do this over the entire circle and also on a strip near the edge, as shown.

5 Now cut out the entire circle then, with the same cutter, cut again to create the shape shown.

6 From the remaining textured paste, cut a strip approx. 8mm x 78mm (⅓ x 3in) wide.

7 Glue the 'hat' to your cupcake dome. Roll a sausage for the hair, twisting into a little 'curl'.

8 Roll a ball to form the bobble of the hat. Flatten slightly then use your toothpick bunch to texturize.

9 Attach the 'hair' first, then the hat band and finally the bobble. Roll a tiny nose, and two black eyes, and attach to face. Add two tiny white non-pareils for the pupils.

10 Add a smile using a brown edible pen. Lightly dusting the cheeks with pink petal dust creates a rosy glow!

11 To create the girl cupcake, follow the steps outlined above to create the face only, and adding tiny little lash details – no hat pieces are required.

12 Cut a strip of pink paste for the headband, and use your quilting tool to add a 'stitched' effect.

13 Attach the hairband at a slight angle and accessorise with a coordinating daisy.

14 Again, add a rosy glow with petal dust to her cheeks. What a cute pair

Birthday Bear

Repeat the steps to make the bear from pages 30-31

1 Make the bear featured on page 40 and use a flower plunger cutter to cut and add some cute little flowers to the head area.

2 For the mini cake, cut 4 circles of paste: 2 pink and 2 brown.

3 Cut 3 more circles, the same size, in white.

4 Use the ball tool and a foam pad to soften the edges of the 2 of the white circles.

5 Stack the layers of cake as show, with the stiff white circle at the bottom.

6 Add the top, frilled white circle as the final 'frosting' layer. Add a small candle holder.

7 Cut a 'slice' from your mini cake.

8 For each balloon, cut 2 circles of the same colour paste.

9 Lay a piece of coated florist wire on top of one circle, half way in.

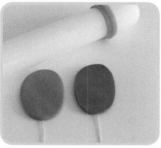

10 Lay the second circle on top, with some glue in between. Roll gently with a rolling pin to merge the two and stretch them into ovals.

11 Cut some small square boxes as gifts. Roll very thin sausages and add 'bow' detail to each gift.

12 For the bunny head and body, roll two fat sausage shapes and indent at one end with your thumb.

13 Roll 2 thin sausages for legs, and 2 shorter ones for arms.

14 Roll and bend 2 smaller ovals for the ears. Glue bunny parts in place under the bear arm, and add black fondant or small black sugar pearls for eyes and nose.

Baby Slippers

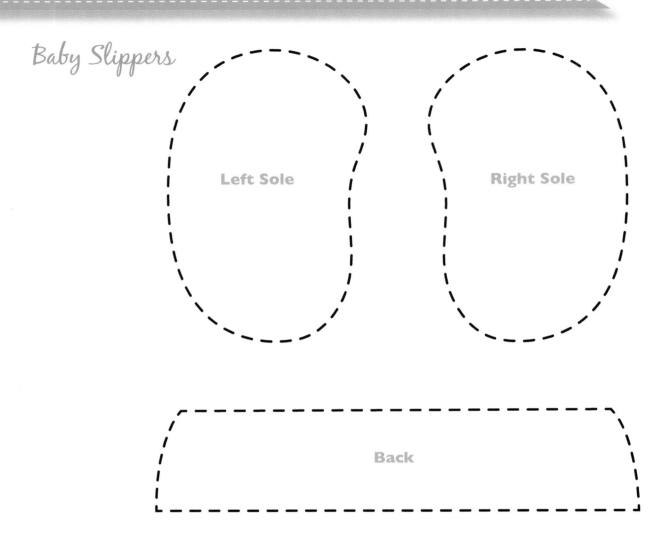

Left Sole

Right Sole

Back

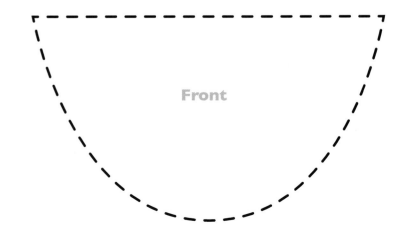

Front

Bunny Cupcakes

Bear Cupcakes

Bib Topper

Onesie Topper

Cupcake

Flower

Star

RECIPES ♥ TUTORIALS

Cake & Bake
ACADEMY
Est. 2014

RESOURCES ♥ INSPIRATION

6509623R00030

Printed in Great Britain
by Amazon.co.uk, Ltd.,
Marston Gate.